# Note To Parents

One way you can help your children learn how to harness the power of their thoughts is by teaching them how to use affirmations.

Positive affirmations offer many different benefits for kids,

including: overcoming negative self-talk, building self-esteem and helping to build the belief that you have the power to create the life you want.

Email us at
coloringbooktafouket@gmail.com
Title the email "Tafouket"
we'll send you
something fun !

# This Book Belongs To:

..............................................................................

# Hi, Little Girl !
## Your thoughts , can become your reality , so speak positive and good to yourself and believe in you .

# I AM CONFIDENT

# I AM BEAUTIFUL

I REACH MY GOAL'S

# Tips for using positive affirmations

- Experiment with different times to use them: when you wake up, before you go to sleep, in the shower, on the ride to school
- Write affirmations down in different places to use as helpful reminders
- Use the list as inspiration to create affirmations that are personal to you
- Make sure they feel natural to you and like something you'd say
- Repeat them a lot! Repetition is important for controlling your monkey mind!

69499343R00026